LARRY D. BARNES
Live a Life Getting What You Want

Published by

3108 E. 10th St.
Trenton, MO 64683

Copyright © 2014, by Vincent Harris

All rights reserved. No part of this book may be reproduced or transmitted in any form by any means, electronic or mechanical, including photocopying, recording, or by any information storage and retrieval system, without the written permission of the publisher, except where permitted by law.

ISBN:978-0-9847952-5-3

Library of Congress Cataloging-in-Publication Data

Harris, Vincent

Larry D. Barnes: Live a Life Getting What You Want, by Vincent Harris

Library of Congress Control Number: 2014918131

Printed in the United States of America

Prologue

The book you hold in your hands is laid out a little differently than most. This book is about the life and times of Larry D. Barnes, but it's not going to be presented in a chronological sequence, beginning with Larry's early life, and coming up through the present day. I didn't know that when I first started working on the book, but after having published four other books, one thing I've learned is that a book takes on a life of its own as it starts coming together. It develops a personality, of sorts, and this personality lends itself to guiding how the book should be structured.

I met with Larry each week over the course of a year. We never spent less than two hours together, and we often spent as many as five or six hours chatting, maybe over a delicious dinner that Diane Barnes—Larry's daughter—had prepared, or while sipping on a glass of wine. Larry told stories, and I asked questions.

We talked of many things, often getting completely off topic, things like politics, the environment, and a couple of Larry's favorite topics—hunting and fishing—but we always worked our way back to the stories of his life. We talked about the stories that were triggered by something in another story Larry was telling, or by something I might have said. In other words, our time together was simply real life conversations between two friends—without any pre-defined sense of structure or organization. We just talked—period.

As the book started coming together, it became more and more obvious that this was also how the book should be formatted. It should flow from one story into another. Just like the conversations, one story might be from the 1970's, and be followed by a story from the 1950's, which would flow into a story from the 1980's. That's how conversations happen, and that's how this book happened, as well.

The stories, of course, and the lessons contained within them, are all related. They are all a part of the proverbial thread that was woven through Larry's life. There is another reason for formatting the book in this manner. As a social scientist, with an undergraduate degree in education, I've always written with one question in mind: How can I present this idea or concept in a way that has the best chance for making it into the long term memory of the reader.

The human brain does not do well when it doesn't have closure. The soap operas know this, and it is one reason an episode did not end with you getting to find out whether "John kissed Sally," or didn't. They knew that leaving that loop open would cause your unconscious mind to process the question "did he kiss her" right up until the time you watched the next episode the following day. And, of course, people did watch the next day.

The format of this book, then, can be thought of as a series of open-ended stories. Each story leaves you with the knowledge that there is more, or perhaps, more you should have known before you just read the story you just finished, and that is the kind of unconscious processing that moves information from short-term memory to long-term memory. Let's face it, if you can't remember it, it's a lot less useful than if you can.

So, read, absorb, and enjoy taking in the nuggets of wisdom offered by one of the most successful men I've ever had the opportunity to get to know.

~ Vincent Harris

Table of Contents

The Beginning	7
The Midas Touch is Born	8
The Art of Selling Fans	12
Perception Becomes Reality	18
When a House is Not a House	23
Using the Strengths of Others	27
The Principle of the Matter	31
Haircuts: Problem or Solution?	35
Winning Everything and Then Some	41
Assumption Equals Limitation	46
Never Let a Good One Get Away	51
The One Thing a Test Can't Measure	56
A Lesson in Leverage	61
The Average Man Syndrome	66
What It Takes to Become a Leader	71
Singing Your Way to Success	76
The Power of Goals	80
Insights from the Writings of Larry D. Barnes	86
Words of Praise for Larry	90
Final Thoughts from the Author	110
Contributions to the Community	113
Chronological History	114

Larry engaged in his favorite hobby.

Larry with the kind of bass he likes to catch-a big one.

The results of a good day of fishing.

Larry's fishing cabin while being constructed. His home away from home.

Larry posing with a large Russian Wild Boar he took with his bow.

The hunting guide standing with a nice Black Bear taken by Larry on a bow hunt.

The Beginning
In the Words of Larry D. Barnes

The depression is easing more each day. "It is extremely hot every day and only three more months of this pregnancy," my mother must have been thinking. Finally, on the 6th of October, 1936, a boy was born—me.

My Dad's mother, Effie, wanted to name me John Henry. Better ideas prevailed, and my name was to be Larry Dale Barnes. I was the fourth child for my parents, the second boy. Two more children were in their future, for a total of six children.

Growing up with five children taught you to get along with other people as well as how to share. We were poor, but we didn't realize how poor we were. There were people in the neighborhood who worked for the railroad and they seemed rich; they made good money. Work, work, work was the seeming order of everyday. There was a war on, and everyone took a part in helping out.

The Midas Touch is Born

"The delicate balance of mentoring someone is not creating them in your own image, but giving them the opportunity to create themselves."

—Steven Spielberg

A young man is just a young man; that is, until he becomes something more, something more clearly defined than just a "young man." What defines that young man? That's not always an easy question to answer. First, of course, it depends on who the young man in question happens to be. There can be multiple variables involved, an almost unlimited number of factors. However, sometimes it's incredibly simple to pinpoint just where, when, and how a given young man began the transformation from "young man" to something that would be more the words "young man" could ever capture.

When the "young man" being discussed is Larry D. Barnes, we can discuss the moment he was defined in great detail, and we will be doing just that in the pages that follow. With youth comes the potentially wonderful openness of the unconscious mind. A human being with a mind that is still looking at the world and asking, "Who am I?"

If that young person happens to be in a home where they experience daily abuse, for example, they may very well determine that "who they are" is less than most other people. Sometimes, though, a young person can have a simple chance encounter that can set a very positive and uplifting tone for the rest of their life.

When Edna Stewart looked at Larry D. Barnes on that evening as he walked her home, and spoke the words "Larry, you have the Midas Touch" a powerful force was set into motion. Who was Edna Stewart? She was a woman who worked in the upstairs offices at the Kress Store where Larry worked as a stock boy. He and Edna—who was many years his senior—would usually walk home together each evening, as they didn't live too far from one another, and they enjoyed each other's company. She wasn't his boss, or even his manager. She was simply a co-worker and a friend, and Larry respected her enough that her words mattered.

Now, we could spend an eternity asking a few questions without ever really knowing the answer:

1. Did she see something that resonated in Larry already that was consistent with the thinking and skills that would create the real world equivalent of "The Midas Touch?"

2. Did the fact that she told Larry D. Barnes he had "The Midas Touch" cause him to begin shaping himself (because he believed her) through the beliefs about himself that he would adopt, and build on throughout the rest of his life?

3. Did this simple statement have such an impact on Larry, that his strong mind drove him to earn 1.4 million dollars each year as a salary, throughout most of his 50's?

The most accurate thing we can say, if we want to say anything at all about the "truthfulness" of the aforementioned possibilities, is that they both probably played a role. Whether that is true, or whether only one of them played a significant role is really a moot point.

The bottom line is that whether it was the first one, the second, or even both, her comment was a catalyst that would play a role in the creation of the kind of wealth that would allow Larry D. Barnes to contribute to the world around him in a significantly measurable way, which would become part of the legacy he would leave behind.

My Thoughts and Reflections on the Section I Just Read

The Art of Selling Fans

"Pretend that every single person you meet has a sign around his or her neck that says, 'Make me feel important.' Not only will you succeed in sales, you will succeed in life."

—Mary Kay Ash

Rules: it might be fair to say that Larry's understanding of rules was that they were concepts to serve as guidelines, but not something to etch in stone and apply to all situations at all times. There would be, as Larry would demonstrate many times throughout his life, times when the rules that governed a particular situation simply did not make sense, and didn't serve anyone in a useful way.

One scorching Missouri summer, long before air conditioning was something you would find in just about every home, Larry's store sold out of fans; not just box fans, but any fan that would move air over a human body and make an otherwise oppressive and energy-sapping day, considerably more tolerable. The heat wave had caused a run on fans.

None of the stores in the local area had much more to offer than one of those shoulder shrugs that says, "Sorry,...I'd love to help you, but no fans means no fans," and a polite "Hopefully we'll be getting some soon. You might check back next week."

"You might check back next week" was not something that was acceptable to Larry. When customers were hot and wanted a fan to cool themselves off, you should be able to sell them a fan. Besides, he was a store manager in Marshall, Missouri that ran a profitable store; the more profitable the better, and how can you make more of a profit selling the fans that people want, if you don't have the fans?

Now, standard operating procedure for this chain of stores—as it was, and still is, for many chains today—was to order them from the warehouse. Of course, because the warehouse provided merchandise for several stores, orders that came in were examined. And, if something was in low supply at the warehouse, a partial order would be sent, so as not to run out and not be able to provide any of the other stores with fans.

Something that you come to know about Larry D. Barnes, right away, is that while he has a gentleness and kindness that could warm the wax right off of a wick, he has a competitive side as well, and this competitive side understands one word: Win.

You see, the gentle side of Larry couldn't stand seeing customers having to sit in sweltering houses, praying for a breeze to wash through the small wire squares of the window screens and slow the pace of at least some of the trickles of sweat that slid down their brows.

Larry cared about his customers. However, the competitive side of Larry didn't care so much for his competitors' customers, as he did his own. And, when it came to how his store measured up against the others in his region, he wasn't about to let some silly operating procedure for the requisition of fans get in the way of selling as many fans as his customers wanted to buy.

With the mercury in the thermometer still pushing into the "miserable" zone each day Larry took his truck, and a driver, and drove to the manufacturer. He wasn't going to wait the period of time it would take for that order to be processed, or run the risk that they fill only a partial order, leaving him with far fewer fans than it would take to cool off the people he knew depended on him for so many of the household items that made their lives easier.

He also knew that as a store manager, who was there himself looking at these men eyeball to eyeball, that they would be much more likely to say "How many do you want?" and less likely to give him the "You can only have THIS many" run around.

Larry's fan rendezvous went off without a hitch; well, at least until the home office found out that he had driven to the manufacturer himself and driven a truckload of fans back to his store, rather than doing things by the rules, or the standard operating procedure. "You can't do that!" the home office manager gruffly assured him. Larry didn't miss a beat.

He knew otherwise. He knew he could do that, and did; he had already sold all of them. His customers were beaming, smiling ear to ear as they came in the door like Water Buffalo that had been roaming the Savannah for days in search of water with no luck, and then, when they had all but given up hope, had stumbled into a life giving Oasis. Larry created an Oasis while everyone else played by the rules and said "Sorry, we're out of fans."

When Larry told me this story his eyes twinkled and he chuckled; that kind of look and laugh that says, "That's why I had such a profitable store. I was willing to do whatever needed to be done to make things happen, and I did. Others weren't, and didn't." Larry would never be so brash as to say it like this, though.

He communicated it only through implication, letting me figure out what he was thinking myself. Larry has a way of making this rather simple to do. He communicates, both verbally and non-verbally, in a way that leaves little on the table. You feel it, and you have a very clear understanding of where his thinking is coming from.

Rules: Chances are good that like most, you are all for rules that are in your favor, or rules you have created, and might even argue that rules, period, are to be followed. Yet, again, if you are like most, when the bending of a rule might serve you well, like getting you in to see the doctor an hour earlier, rather than spending that time in the waiting room, you are probably willing to argue that, here, an exception can be made. Larry understood this as well as anyone, and in a way that few do.

His understanding of when the bending of rules or guidelines was acceptable was far from being self-centered. He drove to get the fans, not just to keep his store on top (although this was also a factor), but because he cared about his people. He cared about "Mrs. Smith" and "Mr. Jones," the people who came to his store when they could have gone elsewhere. They trusted him, and when you placed your trust in Larry D. Barnes, you knew that he'd go out of his way to make you glad that you did.

An interesting thing happened after the fan debacle. Larry was promoted to the largest store in the district, Galesburg, Illinois. Larry was sent to Galesburg to run out the lease, as the store was not making a profit. Upon arriving, Larry started studying the situation, and got right to work on the problems that the store had been having.

Within a short period of time, the store was making money; it was finally making a profit once again, so the home office decided they would remodel the store Larry had brought back to life.

A new district manager was appointed, and he and Larry soon thereafter butted heads. He was going to make changes in Larry's store, undoing many of the changes that Larry had implemented during his rebuilding of the stores financial status. Larry vehemently opposed this. When it became apparent that the district manager was not going to budge, Larry resigned, becoming an agent for an insurance company. This was the start of Larry D. Barnes becoming an insurance man who was bound to succeed. That district manager didn't know it, but he had just paved the way for a man to become a multi-millionaire.

My Thoughts and Reflections on the Section I Just Read

Perception Becomes Reality

"There are things known and there are things unknown, and in between are the doors of perception."

—Aldous Huxley

When you sit across from Larry and he begins telling you a story about something, he manages to pull you into his world. It's like you suddenly realize that while your "circle" may be okay and quite comfortable, the silent invitation he extends to you, inviting you to step into his "circle," is just too compelling.

Without any awareness of exactly when it might have happened, at some point you realize you are in a different place than you were a few moments ago. And while "different" usually puts us off balance at first, "difference," when it relates to leaving your "circle" and stepping into Larry's "circle," can best be described as "coming home."

It shouldn't come as a surprise, then, to learn that Larry D. Barnes didn't hear "no" too often when he was selling insurance door to door. It wasn't because he had a better product than everyone else; he sold the same policy that everyone in his company was selling, or trying to sell.

It wasn't some unfair advantage that allowed him to insure so many people, people who had been absolute strangers less than ninety minutes before they signed their policy application and wrote a check. It was something else. It was an attitude.

Were there other agents who sometimes thought that Larry had some "magic" trick up his sleeve that allowed him to write new business where others couldn't? You had better believe they did. Larry was very much aware of this, and more importantly, perhaps, he was aware of how this erroneous belief could destroy morale among the other agents.

As long as they thought the reason was that someone was outperforming them was because of something beyond their control, there would be no logical reason for them to work to do better.

After hearing a fellow agent complain that the town he was working at the time was "...without any solid prospects to talk to..." Larry decided to show them how outrageous that idea really was. The agent, who had complained, had been out knocking on doors for several days in the little town he was complaining about, and hadn't written a single policy.

At the end of the following week, Larry had insured fifty new people; over four dozen people had signed the application, and then unfolded their vinyl checkbook and carefully signed their name to a check.

The math on this is staggering to say the least. Even if we are looking at a twelve-hour workday, if Larry insured ten people a day, that is still an unreal accomplishment.

Think about this for a moment. Let's pretend that your friend's daughter has sold a fairly big bunch of Girl Scout cookies, and when the cookies come in, a few weeks later, they ask you to help deliver them.

They give you fifty different orders from fifty different people. Keep in mind, these have already been sold, all you have to do is drop them off. Most people will agree that just delivering cookies to fifty different people would take up a good portion of the week—if not the entire week.

During the week Larry sold those fifty policies, he met well over fifty strangers, gained the trust of enough of them to have at least fifty of them let him in to present his product, and of those, fifty of them picked up the pen, signed their name, signed the check, and shook Larry's hand. In fact, Larry didn't recall hearing a single "no" that week.

Over a half a century later, Larry still straightens up in his chair when he tells this story. It's as if he's gained enough distance on this week that when he looks back at what he was able to do on that amazingly productive week, it's as though he is listening to what someone else has accomplished. It's like watching the realization slam down on the table in front of him so hard, and in such an enigmatic way that even Larry goes "Wow. That really is amazing!"

This little town in Illinois that was seemingly "...without

any solid prospects to talk to..." was just another town to Larry. Towns had people. And people had needs, fears, and desires, and they wanted peace of mind. At least that is how Larry looked at it. Whether it was "this" town, or "that" town, "these" people, or "those" people, it was all the same to Larry. He found their need, and then helped them get what they needed.

The mistake that the other agents had made was in looking at a town as being a "good" town or a "bad" town. Once they had lumped any given town into the "bad" category, the impact this mental error would have on their performance and ability to sell was incredibly destructive.

Unfortunately, once this occurs, it spreads to other agents just as assuredly as any virus you might think of—maybe even faster than a virus. Larry D. Barnes was like the long-awaited antibiotic that came along at just the right time to stop the spread of some insidious disease. Through his refusal to buy into the idea that a town could be "good" or "bad," he simply went out and did what he always did.

I don't think it would be a mistake to say that many decades after Larry wrote more new business in five days than most agents would in a month or two that the agents who were there at the time have often recalled the lesson offered that week: Be careful what you believe because it will become true for you once you really believe it. So, make sure that if you are going to believe in something that it is something that will be beneficial to both yourself and others. Believing in "good" towns and "bad" towns isn't good for you, or the people who need to be insured by you.

My Thoughts and Reflections on the Section I Just Read

WHEN A HOUSE IS NOT A HOUSE

"There are no rules of architecture for a castle in the clouds."

—Gilbert Chesterton

During the years, Larry and his Dad used to enjoy lunch together from time to time. They would gaze out the windshield of Larry's car, and engage in easy father and son conversation about some interesting, or even not so interesting topic of the day. On this particular day, they were parked near the southwest end of the upper lake in Trenton, Missouri watching the construction of what could only be described as an "enormous" home.

The home—if you could call it just a "home"—looked to be more along the lines of something you would build for a public venue. Larry said to his Dad, "Who would ever need a home that big?" as he unhurriedly shook his head in disbelief. The home was being built by one of the finest builders in the area, Carl LeBlanc.

Over time, the beliefs that one holds about what is possible...or even reasonable in life can change and expand. They can change, but all too often adult men and women will go through life with the same beliefs and concepts about reality. These are beliefs that yield the same limitations from one decade of life to the next.

For most men in their thirties, for example, who would look at a home like this being built, and think, "Who would ever need a home that big?" a home of that size would never be on their radar as a possibility in their life, not in their thirties, their forties, their fifties...ever. In short, a home that was "too big" would stay put as a home that was "too big." This would not be the case for Larry, however.

When Larry later purchased this home and was having the custom bar designed and built in the lower half of the home he once deemed as "too big" for anyone's needs, he was looking at the evidence of a belief that had been transformed. No longer was his mind thinking, "Who would ever need a home that big?"

No, his mind had long ago dropped the previous limitation, and had stretched its former boundaries to a new, and a much more spacious and distant horizon, a horizon that included one very large and fine-looking home.

When Larry was telling me this story, he chuckled as he said, "When Robert Cullers—his banker—came to look at the home, he said 'Larry, this isn't a home...it's an ESTATE!'"

So what happened? How did Larry go from someone who thought the size of this house was bordering on ridiculous to someone who said, "I am going to buy this house!"? In this case, "happened" is a good term to describe the transition. You see, it was never a decision, per se, on Larry's part. He never said, "Okay, I want to be able to have a big house; I want to create a belief that will allow me to buy a big house."

It "happened" for the most part very *unconsciously* because of the absolutely *conscious* decision Larry had made to continually be learning. To be listening to successful men and women and learning from them. As Larry continued setting goals, hitting them, and then setting new ones, his income had sky rocked over time.

He wasn't focused on an "enormous" house. He was focused on his business...and on himself. The home he purchased was simply something that he had one day realized he could own, and that it would be useful for hosting agency parties for his agents, or simple events for family and friends. So, he bought it.

Of course, there is also the matter of feeling that he deserved the house at the time he made the purchase. There is a correlation between the number of people someone knows they have helped, or the impact they have made on others, and the space that opens up emotionally and psychologically in a person to make room for something bigger and better in their life.

It's not that we can't buy something "big and bold" before we have made a difference, but there is a kind of inner pushback against something that we don't believe (on the unconscious level) we deserve, or that we have earned. When we have that inner alignment, not only is it possible, and easier to get, but it becomes exponentially more trouble-free to keep. This is where Larry had found himself, in a place where he believed he could *want* a home that large, that he could *have* a home that large, and that he *deserved* a home that large.

My Thoughts and Reflections on the Section I Just Read

USING THE STRENGTHS OF OTHERS

"Surround yourself with the best people you can find, delegate authority, and don't interfere as long as the policy you've decided upon is being carried out."

—Ronald Reagan

Intelligence matters, but not necessarily in the way we have been conditioned to think it does. Larry was tested in the Army and has a high I.Q. of 134. All things being equal, an I.Q. of 134 is better than an I.Q. of 114. But see, all things are never equal; the only time "all things are equal" when comparing one human being to another, is in a theoretical sense...in examples we make up.

When we begin to look at other descriptions of "intelligence," we find there are many. So many, in fact, that we could spend days looking and thinking about them all, and running ourselves ragged asking, "Which one is right?" The question that we want to ask is, "Which one is the most useful?" The answer to that question leads to maximizing our abilities, and gets us to not waste time worrying about "rightness" and focusing on "usefulness." This is the difference that makes the difference. It is also the difference that made the difference for Larry D. Barnes.

Larry knew how to leverage others. He knew how to find someone who could do what he could not, or who could do what he could do, but better, or more efficiently, and then hired them to work for him. This is the hallmark of nearly every successful businessman or woman you will ever study.

Fern Shipley is a name that comes to mind. Now, I don't know that Fern had much more than a high school education, Larry didn't say, and it is irrelevant, really. I personally remember Fern, as she was a friend of my Mother, and she was Larry's secretary. Fern was not just any secretary, though. She was a secretary who knew almost everyone in the town of Trenton, Missouri. Who better to introduce Larry to the people who he didn't yet know all that well?

Through one lunch outing after another, Larry and Fern would walk into a local restaurant with Fern stopping to say, "Oh, Hi, John. I'd like you to meet my boss, Larry D. Barnes," and one by one, Fern introduced Larry to everyone she knew. Oh, Larry was more than capable of introducing himself to the people he'd like to become better acquainted with, but why do that?

He knew, all too well, the unparalleled power of third party introductions. The person Fern was introducing him to already knew and trusted Fern, and because they did, there was a sort of transference of trust that went to Larry. A third party introduction can literally shave months, even years, off the time it takes to form a close relationship with someone you have just met.

So, let's get back to intelligence. Larry could have said, "You know, I'm going to do this all by myself. I will go out and introduce myself to people and build relationships with them." But he didn't. He said, "Who do I know that already knows most everyone, and how can I incorporate them so I can meet more people in less time, and close the gap between 'stranger' and 'friend' in the quickest way possible?" That is the kind of "most useful" intelligence I referred to earlier.

Fern Shipley was a microcosm of what Larry was doing elsewhere on a much larger scale. Larry could sell as well as anyone, and better than most anyone if we are going to be precise. But no matter how good someone is, how much can one person really sell? Time becomes a very limiting factor, at some point, creating a metaphorical ceiling that will cap results just as assuredly as any concrete ceiling could.

Larry had developed an understanding of the importance of leverage for getting what he wanted in life. Leverage was the one thing that he could use to outwit the limitations of time. Something anyone can use for this purpose. Larry knew that at some point the number of hours in a given day would limit the number of policies he could sell in any given day. This was simple math.

Larry would go on to create leverage in a way that would make him a multi-millionaire in a relatively short period of time. If Fern Shipley was leverage, recruiting others would have to be called leverage X 10. I'll discuss Larry's use of this powerhouse strategy in the next chapter.

My Thoughts and Reflections on the Section I Just Read

The Principle of the Matter

"Always vote for principle, though you may vote alone, and you may cherish the sweetest reflection that your vote is never lost."

—John Quincy Adams

When Larry realized that recent changes in how commissions had been restructured at Pioneer Life had cost him about $25,000 in personal revenue, he had to consider how he was going to handle the situation. Larry spoke to Peter Nauert, the CEO of Pioneer Life. He said, "Peter, in looking at the changes that were made, the best I can tell, it cost me about $25,000. You can just write me a check for $25,000. I don't need it, and you'll never miss it."

Peter Nauert picked up the phone and talked to his secretary, who issued the check for $25,000 right then and there. Peter and Larry worked together on many projects. Peter was a mentor to Larry, and Larry respected Peter a great deal.

Now, this wasn't the cashier at the local grocery store who had overcharged Larry seventy-five cents on a pork roast. Peter Nauert was the CEO of the company that would be a major vehicle for much of Larry's wealth. Peter hadn't violated laws, either; the changes that were made were within the letter of the law. Larry just didn't feel the changes were particularly ethical in nature, and therefore was willing to stand his ground on principle alone.

Imagine the conviction in his beliefs that required. Think about working with, or for someone, who has been instrumental in the money you have acquired thus far, and will be in the money you make in the future.

You have lots of money, already, and they have done something that wasn't illegal—you just didn't think it was ethical—and you confronted them, knowing the ripples it might create, all because your values and beliefs in "right and wrong" were that rock solid.

It sounds noble, and is, but would you really do the same, or would you be fearful of how squabbling over a relatively insignificant amount might slow down your ongoing wealth? Most people I asked had to stop and really think about the questions. They said, "You know, I'd like to think I could confront him, but I'd probably just keep quiet and go on, so I didn't risk my wealth!"

During my interviews with Larry in 2013-2014, I had the opportunity to see his tenacity and vigilance when it comes to principles and values. More than once, I sat quietly, just watching and listening, as Larry spoke with one of his lawyers discussing various legal matters that were based on a violation of values.

Moments before one of these calls, Larry would appear almost docile, seated back comfortably in his chair, speaking in a soft, very relaxed voice, and his movements and gestures somewhat slow and measured. His attorney would call, and suddenly Larry's back would straighten. His head would literally rise 3-4 inches as a result. The previously soft and slightly slumped shoulders would pull back, bringing his chest out almost in unison with his jutting jaw. Larry's voice would deepen, and the volume would dial up a few notches.

In defending one of his deeply held values, Larry blossomed. He didn't yell, and he didn't do anything that would border on someone about to lose control because of their anger. No, this was a very focused tenacity. He had emotional control, and kept his outcome clearly in mind. When the phone call was over, Larry would smoothly shift back into the "relaxed and laid-back" Larry D. Barnes. It was an amazing process to watch, and I got to see it several times.

Yes, $25,000 to most of us would be a sizeable amount of money. But, when you are worth several million dollars, not so much. $25,000 is 1/4 of 1/10th of a million dollars, and Larry had several million dollars, so it was literally next to nothing for him. If you were worth $100,000, then 1/4 of 1/10th would be $2,500. Divide that by five (assuming Larry was worth five million dollars at that time) that's $500. Would you risk your $100,000 over $500?

Larry D. Barnes would, and did; he is a man of principle, and a man of his word. From his early beginnings, through his life as it is being lived as I write this book, Larry is a man whose word you can count on. His grade school teachers knew it, his superiors in the Army knew it, his employers knew it, and most importantly, perhaps, regarding his professional life, his agents knew it.

The United States Army had selected Larry as the soldier they wanted to be their Radar Technician. They didn't have the time to send him to the six-month Radar School, so he took his position without the schooling that virtually every other Radar Technician had received, but did a fantastic job anyway. This played a huge role in Larry making the rank of Sergeant at such a young age. As would be the case many times in his life, he had found himself in a less than ideal situation, and not only survived, but in true Larry D. Barnes fashion, he thrived.

My Thoughts and Reflections on the Section I Just Read

Haircuts: Problem or Solution?

"The game of life is a lot like football. You have to tackle your problems, block your fears, and score your points when you get the opportunity."

—Lewis Grizzard

Some people show promise as musicians early in life, while others show a proclivity for mathematics, or science, and sometimes we can see early evidence of men and women who have an eye for opportunities to prosper financially. For anyone who was watching Larry in his early adult life, they would have seen one such example.

While serving in the United States Army, Larry was living in the Army barracks. Each time the announcement of an inspection was made, Larry noticed that many of the men were bellyaching about the cost of having to get the required haircut that would be needed if they had any hopes of passing the inspection.

When Larry went on leave, he purchased a set of Wahl clippers, the kind still used by barbers around the world today. Upon his return, he announced that he would be offering haircuts at half the price that the barber was charging. "I wasn't very good, at first," Larry said with a wry grin, "I goofed up the first few guys pretty good, but I got better as time when on, and they were more than willing to let me do it, so they could save the money."

Right before an inspection, Larry was in the latrine with one GI after another. They were lined up to get their discount haircut. Larry was putting this money aside for another money-making idea, one he would leverage off of the back of his side-line barber job.

See, Larry had also noticed, for some time, that the guys who played poker and gambled were usually out of money a few days before payday. Always itching to get in on these late night poker games, and the camaraderie that went along with it, the only thing that prevented many of them from doing so was a lack of cash.

Larry launched his next venture; he would loan a broke GI ten bucks, today, a few days before payday, for fifteen bucks as repayment on payday. To the man who faced being left out of the Friday and Saturday night poker fest because he was fresh out of cash, he paid Larry five dollars extra, fifteen in total, in a few days in order to have temporary use of Larry's ten dollars, now. Not too surprisingly, Larry was more than happy to oblige.

Now, I should mention that it wasn't quite this streamlined. See, Larry was notified early on that he was not allowed to charge for his hair cutting services, as that would be running a business in the barracks, and that was not allowed. Larry pondered this situation. "If someone offers a donation for something someone has done for them, then that is not a business. That is just something someone did for someone else, and the person who received the good deed felt compelled to offer a donation," Larry thought to himself.

So, what did Larry do? That's right, he simply "recommended" to his Army buddies that it might be a nice gesture if they were to offer a donation of, oh...say one-half of what the barber was charging. Larry was not about to let the opportunity he spotted be brought to an end before it even started because of technicalities. He was far too creative to allow this to happen, and so he didn't.

"I have always been able to make money!" Larry told me as he was reflecting on this story. "I would see a need, and fill it." Larry was made Sergeant while in the Army. At the age of twenty, this made him the youngest sergeant, but also made him a lot more money, which he welcomed.

To get an idea of the effectiveness and depth of Larry's barracks ventures, it might be helpful to share what he was able to do with the money he earned from them. "I paid cash for all of the furniture in my house when I got out," Larry proudly confessed.

That little house, a pink house, situated at 15th and Main, in Trenton, Missouri was the beneficiary of Larry's thinking. It was the beneficiary of his keen awareness and ability to see what others were calling for (whether they knew it or not) and having the wherewithal to capitalize, and provide what others wanted and needed, and to make a nice profit for himself in the process.

Now, was Larry the only one who recognized that others thought the cost of haircuts from the barber were too high, or that the poker players of the barracks would frequently run out of money before payday, but still very much wanted to get in on the games? Not likely, it was probably something that was noticed, commented on, and even laughed about by many other people. The others simply saw it as a condition that existed, but not an opportunity, and therein lies the difference between Larry, and everyone else.

Were there to have been someone else in the barracks who did happen to see it as an opportunity, one thing is clear. They recognized it, and stopped right there. Larry knew that seeing an opportunity and filling the need that opportunity creates are two very different—although connected—things. It's an equation, of sorts. A + B = C. A—Seeing the opportunity/need + B—Implementing a product/service that provides that want/need to those who want/need it = a potential profit.

If we were to ponder, "Why didn't the other men see the same opportunity?" one reason comes to mind pretty quickly. Most people don't see too far beyond their own needs and desires. In short, if the other men had money to play poker, they didn't have a problem.

If they didn't have money to play poker, they were fixated on the idea of finding a way to fund themselves back into playing, and weren't looking at the big picture, which was that people run out of money for poker from time to time, and when we/they do, we/they want the money we/they need to continue. Their focus had only been on themselves, and their return to poker.

Larry may have had another advantage; he wasn't much of a poker player himself, so he wasn't caught up in the emotions of playing/not playing, and was able to see the big picture more easily, perhaps. It might be compared to watching a police car chase on television.

The advantage the person watching it on television has over the police cars trying to catch the evader is the lack of intense emotions and the resulting tunnel vision it creates. The distanced viewing allows for taking in more information, and making considerations from a place of relative neutrality. This was Larry's perspective when it came to spotting the need that had presented itself with the "poker player dilemma."

In summary, Larry did two things that no one else in those barracks was doing:

1. He identified an opportunity to make a profit by spotting a need others had (that was not being filled by someone else—or at least not very effectively).

2. He discovered a way to fill that need, through supplying the service, product, or anything else that might be needed, and charging enough for his doing so to make a profit.

Why doesn't everyone do this? That is the wrong question. Embrace the fact that not everyone does, and see that as the opportunity for you to do as Larry did, and be one of the few who do. The questions you can ask that do matter, and that will be helpful are: When am I going to begin doing this? Where are opportunities already lurking that I may have already spotted? How will I go about delivering the need?

My Thoughts and Reflections on the Section I Just Read

Winning Everything and Then Some

"Call it what you will, incentives are what get people to work harder."

-Nikita Khrushchev

Over the years, countless companies and organizations have offered prizes to their salespeople as incentives. "A Brand New Washer & Dryer to the person with the most sales this week!" the newsletter might read. And, five business days later, someone will be taking home the latest washing and drying technology for their efforts that week (and selling their old set to their brother-in-law who has been out of work, and shoving quarters into the Laundromat washers and dryers like a retiree playing the slot machines in Vegas).

As you might imagine, most companies wind up giving the prizes to a handful of the same people each contest cycle, to the top sales performers of the company. The companies Larry represented got used to giving all of their prizes to one person, however, Mr. Larry D. Barnes. Larry won a piano, a riding lawn mower, a beautiful two-door refrigerator, and virtually always had part of his home furnished with his winnings.

Eventually, he had won every prize ever offered, and some of them more than once. In an attempt to be creative, they awarded

Larry a trip to San Francisco, complete with airfare and a beautiful hotel for him and his wife to enjoy some time on the west coast. This was a stark contrast from the terrain in Winnebago, Illinois, which was where he lived at the time.

One company, in their "infinite wisdom," decided to eliminate Larry from their competitions. "It isn't fair to the other agents," was their thinking "let's give the others a chance." The others had their "chance," and always had; their "chance" had occurred simultaneously with Larry's. He capitalized, and they did not.

Let's examine the impact of this change (keeping Larry out of the competitions) on the other agents. First, think about finding yourself in a group of other men (if you are a man) or women (if you are a woman) and discovering that there will be a "most handsome man" or "most beautiful woman" contest. Then, it is announced that everyone but George, or everyone but Mary (the two most likely most attractive people) will be excluded from the competition.

If you won, knowing that the best looking man or woman had been kept out of the competition, would you really feel like your title or award was legitimate? Of course not—Just like my Navy SEAL instructors used to tell us when I was in Basic Underwater Demolition Training, "Second place is the first place loser!" Not necessarily the most inspirational feeling you can have.

What impact did this have on Larry and how he thought about having competitions and awarding prizes when he had his own agency? It was probably the best thing that could have happened to him. He constantly had some kind of contest running, and the prizes he awarded were nothing to sneeze at. Trips to Hawaii, brand name appliances....the kind of prizes that he knew triggered something in the psyche of his agents, and made them want to go the extra mile, and make one more call, knock on one more door, or ask for the sale one more time.

Larry remembered something that the people who cut him off from the contests never had the insight to ask him. He knew that even though he was a top performer, and won most if not all of the contests he was part of, he knew, without a doubt, that during those contests he put out a little more than he did when there was not a contest. He also knew that even though he won them most of the time, the other agents almost always put out a little more, as well.

In short, all they accomplished by eliminating Larry from the contests was dulling the drive—even if subtly—of one of their top producers. (But, when it comes to a top producer, even subtle differences can mean a lot of money to an agency or company).

Larry D. Barnes had learned one rule of motivation the hard way—and it paid off for him later: You never penalize your top performers for their superior performance. Sales is the one profession where "survival of the fittest" applies as much as anywhere.

When you discover who the "fittest" salespeople are, you reward them. Sure, you'll have agents who get frustrated and quit, and that is probably best. Those agents wind up spreading doom and gloom to others. You never cease taking care of the top salespeople, to try to avoid the risk of losing some of your poorer performers. You just don't.

When I hear "equal opportunity" Larry comes to mind. He provided the very same opportunity to every agent. What they did with that opportunity was up to them. Those who maximized the opportunity were rewarded—plain and simple.

Mark 4:25 "Whoever has will be given more; whoever does not have, even what they have will be taken from them."

My Thoughts and Reflections on the Section I Just Read

Assumption Equals Limitation

"Begin challenging your own assumptions. Your assumptions are your windows on the world. Scrub them off every once in awhile, or the light won't come in"

—Alan Alda

We've all been a little short on cash before payday. It's an almost Universal experience. For most people, this might be three hundred dollars short on the mortgage, or fifty-seven dollars below the required minimum payment on a credit card. How would you like to find yourself needing ninety-two thousand dollars—yes, $92,000—by Friday, just four days prior?

Once the Larry D. Barnes Insurance Agency had really taken off, there was a tremendous amount of cash flow each month. The agency was making more than enough money, but sometimes, when that much money is coming in, and a significant amount of money is going back out, timing can mean everything.

With over 100 agents in the field, selling insurance policies and being paid a commission on those policies that same week, a 48-hour gap between money going out, and the next round of money coming in could create a challenge on occasion.

When Larry and Robert Brown—who was the head of accounting at the agency—discussed the need for $92,000 to cover expenses and getting everyone paid that week Larry said, "We'll go up to the bank and get a loan tomorrow morning!" Robert asked, "What are you going to use for collateral?" "Collateral," Larry asked quizzically, "we won't need any collateral!" Robert Brown scoffed, "Oh...you sure will! They're not going to loan you that much money with no collateral!"

That next morning, Robert Brown climbed into Larry's tan and brown Cadillac, and eased out of the agency parking lot to see Robert Cullers at the Mercantile Bank. Larry strode through the door with his usual confident gait with Robert following behind somewhat less...no, much less confident.

"Good morning, Larry!" Robert Cullers said, as the two men shook hands, while simultaneously giving each other's suit and shined shoes a once over look. "What can I do for you this morning?" Cullers asked. "I need a $92,000 loan for the agency," Larry said, with poise. "It will be in your account tomorrow morning, Larry. Is there anything else I can do for you?" Cullers asked, as he gave Larry the "We appreciate your business" kind of look.

While rising up from his chair, Larry said, "No, that will do it today. Thank you," and touched Brown on the shoulder, much the same way a father would to his young son when he has just demonstrated an important life lesson.

It was a quiet walk to the car. Brown said nothing, and Larry was just as quiet. Once seated inside, just as Larry was turning right back onto 9th street and the pristine brown Cadillac (brown cars had become a trademark of Larry's) accelerated slowly, Brown interrupted the silence. "I would have never have believed it unless I would have seen it—a $92,000 loan with no collateral. I never would have believed it!"

One important concept jumped out immediately as Larry shared this story with me. As involved with the agency and the accounting as Robert Brown was, he knew as much about the agency finances as Larry. He knew what a "cash cow" the agency was, and the literal abundance of money that came in on a monthly basis.

What Larry had that Robert was lacking was an absolute sense of certainty that his personal reputation and integrity coupled with the rock solid backing of his agency would be more than enough reason for the bank to loan him the money.

This, by the way, is why Larry had always been a top salesmen wherever he happened to be. That same poise and self confidence that made Robert Cullers feel comfortable enough to give Larry an unsecured loan for $92,000 was the same confidence that made total strangers feel comfortable enough to write a check and hand it to Larry for health insurance.

One thing is almost certain, had Larry have expressed the same doubt and hesitancy that Brown displayed when he asked Robert Cullers for the loan, he may very well have been needing to put some of his farm ground up as collateral.

The agency was in great financial shape, yes, and that is certainly comforting to a banker. However, just as important, if not more, were Larry's traits, his habits, his consistent actions, and all of the other things that existed, not on paper, but in the man, himself that made other human beings say, "I trust this man," and loan him money.

This occurred in the 1980's, a different time in banking regarding credit and loans, no doubt. What hasn't changed in the last twenty-five to thirty years, however, is the role self-confidence and personal integrity play not only in one's business life, but also in personal lives, as well.

My Thoughts and Reflections on the Section I Just Read

NEVER LET A GOOD ONE GET AWAY

"Paper is to write things down that we need to remember. Our brains are used to think."

—Albert Einstein

When I first started spending time each week, starting in 2013, asking Larry questions and listening to his stories, gathering information for this book, I always showed up with my yellow legal pads. I would write as fast as I could, filling page after page, as I captured every shred he shared. One afternoon, Larry's daughter, Diane, commented, "Dad always had a yellow legal pad with him. Even when I was a kid, I remember him always writing things down on his yellow pads!"

Larry simply nodded as he said, "Yes, I guess that is right. I did always have them with me. I didn't want to allow any idea I might have to escape. I didn't want to have to rely on my memory. I recorded as much as possible so I could free up my mind for thinking!"

When Larry was an agent, recording his thoughts allowed him to become a better salesman. It also allowed him to go from being a salesman to having an insurance agency of his own with over 100 agents.

The events that would eventually transpire during the creation of the agency were first thoughts in Larry's mind. Ideas that had they been allowed to drift away and to escape his awareness may have never have become the instrumental pieces of the puzzle that they eventually did.

The power of the unconscious mind, or, more accurately stated in 2014, the power of unconscious processing, was something that Larry understood, even if only intuitionally. He grasped the concept that his conscious awareness was very limited, and could process small chunks of information only.

Larry also knew that another part of his mind, his unconscious processing, could process an almost infinite amount of information, and, in fact, could and would do much of it even while he was sleeping.

Every now and then, when Larry would be telling me some long ago event from an earlier part of his life, he would excuse himself from the room, and then, suddenly, he would emerge carrying a journal, or yellow legal pad with thoughts he had recorded years before.

Every time I would look at these recorded thoughts, I realized that I was getting a rare glimpse, not of Larry's thoughts about his thoughts back then...but his actual thoughts from back then...just as they occurred. There lies the magic in recording our thoughts: Clarity.

Larry would also draw diagrams for me, another masterful use of his yellow legal pads. Once, while explaining a concept about investing, he slid his pad out in front of me and started drawing.

With a few circles here, a box there, and a series of lines connecting them in a precise manner, he moved the concept from something very abstract to an idea with more of a concrete feel to it, and my understanding instantly deepened.

Let me tell you something else I experienced during Larry's drawings that you might find fascinating. When he used the pen to point something out that he had just drawn, he didn't use it like a pen, or even a pointer; Larry used that pen much the same way a conductor of an orchestra might use their baton to keep the entire symphony flowing.

He would very purposely—so it seemed—raise it up to eye level, and then as gracefully as a swan, lead you to look right where he wanted you to look. It felt like being on an amusement park ride that I very much wanted to be riding on.

Another use of the yellow legal pads, which was also a testimony to his integrity, was how he used them when presenting to people who he had called on while he was an agent working out on the road. It should come as no surprise that when it comes to commission sales there will always be people who will stretch the truth—even lie—in order to make a sale.

Larry made every presentation, and wrote every promise he made, on his trusty yellow pad. The couple would watch as he wrote, and he drew pictures and diagrams. When he was finished, he tore the sheets from the pad, and left it with them. Every claim he made, they had proof of. You have to be straight as an arrow to be able to do that, and Larry did.

If one were able to hold every yellow legal pad that Larry ever etched his ideas upon, starting with the first one he had ever used and ending with the last one he had ever used, you'd have gold; gold in the form of black ink on yellow paper.

One thing we can know, without question, is that for Larry the pads were a launching pad for some pretty remarkable things in Larry's life. Could they be in yours, too?

My Thoughts and Reflections on the Section I Just Read

The One Thing a Test Can't Measure

"The starting point of all achievement is desire."

—Napoleon Hill

Many companies use expensive and sophisticated testing and analysis to try to determine who they should hire, or who would be the most successful salesperson. In 1966, Larry drove to Columbia, Missouri to take a series of tests for a possible job with MFA selling insurance. Larry's brother worked for them, and he thought Larry might be a good fit for the company.

As Larry focused on answering the questions he was being asked, drawing diagrams, doing math problems, and punching holes in various locations on cardboard (all part of the personality assessment), he periodically glanced at the clock to see how long he had been engaged in the seemingly ridiculous and wasteful use of his time.

After toiling all day long, Larry happily made his way back to his car about 5:00 p.m., anxious to get back on the road and clear his head of the convoluted examples and questions he'd been weaving his way through all day.

About a week later, Larry was called into MFA by Bill Convoy to find out what the results of his testing had been. "Larry," Bill said, "It doesn't look like you're cut out for the insurance business."

However, since your brother is with us, we'll give you a shot." That "shot," by the way, found Larry as the top producer, month after month.

Had Larry's brother not worked there, Larry would most likely have been given a limp handshake and a "Thank you so much for coming to MFA seeking employment....please keep us in mind for your insurance needs" parting comment, and that would have been that.

Imagine how easily Larry could have left, thinking, "Wow, those were some very scientific tests, and they determined I was not cut out for insurance. I guess I better look at doing something else!"

Rest assured that over the years many men and women did do that, based on a series of tests that amounted to little more than a wasted day. Many people who would have likely set the world on fire as salespeople walked away with their tail between their legs, awed at the "magnificence" of the tests that "determined" what they could do, and what they could not.

Many years later, when Larry ran one of the most successful agencies in the nation, he remembered the fallacy of the testing used by MFA so many years before. He knew, all too well, there was one thing that no test could measure: desire.

No test that existed could peek down inside and see the psyche of a human being, and know whether they would crumble or rise like a champion when the pressure was on. Only one thing would do that, i.e. allowing someone to get in the middle of the "fight." They will either sink or swim, but no human being can know who will do what beforehand.

Larry had one way of thinking about the recruiting of agents, and his message echoed through the hearts and minds of the managers doing the recruiting for the agency: If there isn't any obvious reason you can find not to hire them, then, go ahead and contract them!

When I asked Larry if he had been surprised over the years by people who may have appeared to have had little chance of succeeding, he told me the following: "Surprised? No, not really surprised. I knew that almost anyone could be the one who would become a top agent, and I'd never know who they were, until it happened. I just had to give enough people a chance, and out of those people, some of them would. That much I was sure of. So, no, I wasn't surprised when it happened!"

Many decades after Larry first took those tests with MFA, there have been countless new tests developed to attempt to spot the "superstars" in the testing centers. To date, they've all proven to be about as worthless as those Larry took so many years ago.

Is that to say they have no merit, or that they have no place in helping to assess human beings in the workplace? No. There are applications where they may prove useful. However, one fact remains—you cannot measure desire.

You cannot tell what another human being will do when the

heat is on, so you should put the heat on them, let them go, and find out that way. It's the only way. Larry knew that, and it played a big part in making him the wealthy philanthropist he became. The world is a better place because of it.

My Thoughts and Reflections on the Section I Just Read

_____

_____

_____

_____

_____

_____

_____

_____

_____

_____

_____

_____

_____

_____

_____

_____

A Lesson in Leverage

"Your workforce is your most valuable asset. The knowledge and skills they have represent the fuel that drives the engine of business - and you can leverage that knowledge."

—Harvey Mackay

There wasn't a lot of money in Larry's house when he was growing up. His father was a builder, and his mother made sure meals were cooked, the house was clean, and did what many strong women of that time did; she kept things and the family functioning and running. Today, in a time when most kids have a phone in their backpack, it's hard to imagine having to try to figure out how you were going to get a wristwatch.

Larry's parents couldn't afford to buy him a watch, and if they could have found a way, they weren't going to be able to do it for all of their children. That was their thinking, at least. Larry was open to alternative methods of getting his watch, some way other than saving for weeks and months, and doing without the watch until he had all the money required.

Larry spotted a Banner 17 Jewel Watch—a fine watch at that time—and one still sought by collectors today. A man by the name of Joe Apacan ran a jewelry store, and offered in store credit for $1.25 a week. Larry could get the watch now, and go ahead and start enjoying it, while paying for it one week at a time. Larry said,

"I had that watch for many years. I was proud that I had bought and paid for it myself!"

This watch represented two key learning points early in Larry's life: An awareness and utilization of the concept of credit, and the experience of giving someone his word that he would follow through on paying for something, even though he already had the merchandise.

Credit, as Larry would discover later, was an essential part of living in the 20th Century, and would become even more so as time went on. This was true, for men and women who had normal "9-5" "clock-punching" jobs, but particularly true for those venturing into business for themselves.

Larry also understood the connection between credit, and the commitment one makes when they buy something on credit, and having to work enough to make sure that you can keep that commitment. Today, many people mistakenly see credit as a tool they can use so they don't have to work as much.

In the summer, he mowed yards, and not the way a teenager might today. He didn't have a power mower to use—few people did. In the winter, Larry braved the cutting wind and subzero temperatures, and shoveled snow in driveways. He said, "I mowed yards and shoveled snow, yes, but I did about anything I could do to make money!" Larry was speaking of a time period between the ages of 10 and 12 years old.

Later, he bought a bicycle on credit, once again paying $1.25

a week. He said, "It seemed like it took forever to pay it off. I worked very hard to clean it and keep it clean. When I showed it to my Dad, he said 'It looks nice, but the rims need cleaning!'" His Dad helped instill the idea that if you were going to do something, do it all the way, don't just do part of it "right," do it all that way. Larry commented on this lesson and others from his Dad saying, "These little lessons stack up to give you the complete package!"

A strong work ethic is something Larry promoted vigorously at the Larry D. Barnes Insurance Agency. Let's be clear about something, going out and knocking on doors and introducing yourself to total strangers, seeking to sell them an insurance policy is not for the weak minded.

Most agents will hear "No!" a lot more than they hear "Yes!" and this applies to every stage of the process from the greeting at the door, and an attempt to get inside, to asking for the sale after presenting the policy.

Rejection, or feeling like you've been rejected, and how well you can handle that and keep going will test you like few other things in life. If your work ethic is weak, you'll likely crumble. If your work ethic is strong, you at least have a chance. Without it, you are doomed.

One of Larry's favorite ways to put things in perspective and to help promote a stronger work ethic was to call his agents together and ask them about the worst thing they experienced that week. When an agent, for example, would say, "Well, one lady screamed 'Get out of here, don't ever come back' and then slammed the door in my face!" Larry would reply, with a healthy streak of sarcasm,

"Oh, my! I'll bet that was terrible. How on earth did you get through the rest of the day? Are you okay? Are you hurt? That is awful!" Of course, Larry had a flair for using sarcasm and simultaneously conveying deep respect and a desire to help you become better.

Now, as you might imagine, if you were the agent Larry was saying this to, about your "worst thing that happened," it would suddenly sound utterly ridiculous. This, of course, was the desired effect, and it was just one of many tools Larry used to help a struggling salesman tighten up his mind, and thus, his work ethic.

That Banner 17 Jewel watch was more than just a watch; it was a timepiece and a symbol of powerful life lessons.

My Thoughts and Reflections on the Section I Just Read

_____

_____

_____

_____

_____

_____

_____

_____

_____

_____

_____

_____

_____

_____

The Average Man Syndrome

"The difference between average people and achieving people is their perception of and response to failure."

—John C Maxwell

In the early 1970's, Larry sold success programs for a company in Denver, Colorado. Here, he was exposed to the concept of "The Average Man Syndrome," and he would use this as a teaching model for the rest of his business life.

He used it to effectively convey to those looking for a new career that men and women, who became wealthy working for a salary, or an hourly wage, were as rare as hen's teeth. The way to wealth was selling on commission and/or having your own business that incorporates the same strategy.

Larry would enthusiastically say, "The average man will stand out in the rain for 2 hours to get a $10 an hour job. That's $400 a week before taxes." (The figures have been adjusted to those typical with 2014).

But, let's look at what the average man wants in life. He wants a good reliable car. What does that cost? $15,000 is probably a good number to go with. He wants a nice home. What does a good home cost? Does it cost $100,000? Folks, we are talking about having those things on $400 a WEEK, and we haven't even talked about groceries yet, or the light bill.

The fact is, the average man wants those things, but cannot have them working for a salary or an hourly wage. There is only one, reliable way I know that this can happen to anyone willing to work hard enough—selling on commission.

Larry gave this presentation, hundreds of times, perhaps. Each time, some young person would catch a glimpse of the truth Larry was talking about. They would see something that they had never had anyone else tell them: that it was possible to become wealthy without a college degree, or without having an exceptional I.Q.

They could, in fact, make as much money as they wanted to make by providing a service or product that others wanted and/or needed.

Now, it's important to understand the resistance, and the push back that this idea had, and always will have, among the masses. The fact is most people do work for a salary or an hourly wage. And, to hear that you can likely never become wealthy working like this is something you just would not want to hear.

You'd likely seek the few examples in the world where people have become wealthy as a salaried employee and say, "That is bunk! Look at THIS guy! He was on salary and look what he did!" Of course, there are those examples, but they are few and far between. Sales has long been and will long remain one of the highest paid professions in the world.

Can you imagine the young man who has just graduated high school, who has been planning on going to college, coming home and saying, "Mom, Dad....I'm not going to school. I'm going to sell insurance!"? The response of most parents was predictable. "What? Are you crazy? You can't sell! You need a stable job!"

Sadly, many men and women caved in, took that "stable" job, and are still reluctantly dragging themselves in each morning, almost nauseated when they think about how many years they have left before they can retire. That's the average man...and staying there is the average man syndrome. Larry was not an average man, nor was he looking for average men.

If you are reading this, and have a salaried position, or work for an hourly wage, you might be thinking, "Wait a minute! I am relatively happy. I make decent money. I'm not rich, but I have enough for what I want to do in life."

Who is Larry D. Barnes, or anyone, for that matter, to tell me what I need to do to be successful in life? Larry would be the first to tell you, if you are happy with what you do, by all means, keep doing it, and congratulations; so many people do not enjoy what they do. You are fortunate.

So many people, however, are not happy with their lot in life. They are working in a job they don't like. They are living in a home or apartment (or with their parents) that is an environment that does not make them look forward to coming home. Many are driving a car that breaks down frequently, or they at least have the fear of it doing so.

They think that taking vacations to interesting and exotic places are just things that other people get to do. They have hobbies that require the use of some kind of instrument or tool, etc., and they use borrowed or discount stuff (junk) and envy those who can afford high quality equipment.

These are the people Larry talked to; those who wanted something more in life, than what they had, and didn't know how to go about getting what they wanted. The average man syndrome was a metaphor they could grasp.

It was something that defined their current predicaments and the "trapped" feelings they had been experiencing. More importantly, it provided powerful clues that would serve for one to find the exit from the self-imposed trap, and into a life that they desired.

My Thoughts and Reflections on the Section I Just Read

WHAT IT TAKES TO BECOME A LEADER

"A good leader takes a little more than his share of the blame, a little less than his share of the credit."

—Arnold Glasow

"I'm going to create the position of a State Manager," Larry D. Barnes said with a cool and calm but electrifying tone of voice. "He'll fly on our plane several times a month. He'll have a very handsome salary, and a generous expense account; he'll be a leader that others in the agency look to for advice and motivation." The group of men Larry was speaking to were riveted to every word that mellifluously echoed from Larry as he painted glorious pictures in their heads. This was in 1983.

Some of the men longed for a position like the one Larry described, but for as bad as they might be aching for that kind of lifestyle, at that moment, they simply didn't believe they had what it would take to do, what would be required of someone with that much responsibility. One of the young men in the room that day felt something compellingly irresistible churning deep within him. The proverbial kindling of his soul had been sparked by the emotional intensity of Larry's words.

Later that day, a lanky young man with thinning surfer-blonde hair approached Larry. "I want that position! I want to be the State Manager!" Dan McNerney had been with the Larry D. Barnes

Insurance Agency for a short time, but was certain that this was where he wanted to be.

"Dan," Larry said, after pausing a few seconds to let Dan's words settle in. "There is something important to know about becoming a leader. In order to become an effective leader, you have to be able to take direction from others, and demonstrate your ability to follow through with what you are asked to do. If you truly want to become the State Manager, you show me that you can follow effectively, and we'll go from there!"

Dan McNerney took Larry's challenge; he applied himself with a "childlike faith," as Dan would tell me when we discussed his journey from a field agent to the State Manager of the Larry D. Barnes Insurance Agency. During a conversation between Dan and me, Dan reflected on his mindset at the time. He said, "Larry told me that if I was willing to be knocking on the first door at 9:00 a.m. and be knocking on the last door at 5:00 p.m., or later, and would master the basics, I could become a successful agent and have a shot at becoming the State Manager. Who was I to question someone as successful as Larry?"

Larry was not looking for someone who looked like a leader. He was not necessarily looking for the top producing agent to become the State Manager. He was not looking for the most popular agent among his peers. All of these things counted, of course, in their own way, in a cumulative kind of way. What Larry was looking for, above all else, was someone who could carry out his requests to the letter. He found that in Dan McNerney. Dan became the State Manager in 1984.

Now, to set the stage appropriately for highlighting the significance of Dan's rise from field agent to State Manager, it might be useful to reveal the account balance in Dan's checking account his first week in the field. He had $67 and not a dime more. Because each agent was responsible for his motel expenses, gas, meals, etc., Dan knew he barely had enough to see him through the first week.

Dan shared the following with me over a meal of T-bone steaks at Larry's, in July of 2014: "At the end of my first week on the road as an agent, I was driving back home, thinking about the fact that I had earned over $700 in commissions that week. I had never really made much more than $200 a week prior to that. I was overcome with emotion, and literally had to pull over and let the tears of joy flow for a few minutes. I knew I had found what I was meant to do!"

Years later, as State Manager, just as Larry had promised he would do for the person holding that position, Dan was living the life of an executive. He was earning $250,000 a year, was given a company car, had a handsome expense account, and frequently boarded the agency plane to conduct business around the state of Missouri. $250,000 would be a generous salary in 2014, but the money Larry paid Dan in 1984 would be the equivalent of approximately $750,000 a year in 2014. To put that into perspective, the President of the North Central Missouri College is paid somewhere in the neighborhood of $120,000-$140,000 a year, and no doubt has something that resembles an expense account, or a housing stipend, etc. This is a very comfortable arrangement, and one well deserved by the President of NCMC, who has done great things for the college, but Dan's salary, in today's figures, was in excess of one half million dollars more than what the President of the college was making. A phenomenal income in any geographical area in the United States let alone rural north central Missouri.

Dan told me that he has always used Larry's template for finding potential leaders. "I tell others, just as Larry told me, that to become a great leader, you must first demonstrate the ability to follow. It's a simple formula, and Larry was a huge advocate of mastering the fundamental things. I have found it to be as valuable today, as it was thirty years ago!"

Dan McNerney didn't set out to recreate the wheel, as many often do in their attempt to impress someone and gain a favorable position. No, Dan simply did what Larry suggested. He showed that he could follow simple directions, and do so consistently. If the directions were so simple to follow, why didn't everyone do so? While the directions were simple to follow, they were also simple not to follow, and for many agents, they proved even simpler to not do, than to just go ahead and do. That, as much as anything, was the difference that made the difference for Dan McNerney.

My Thoughts and Reflections on the Section I Just Read

Singing Your Way to Success

"Words mean more than what is set down on paper. It takes the human voice to infuse them with deeper meaning."

—Maya Angelou

Have you ever watched a movie where the members of a chain gang who were working on the roads in Mississippi were singing a song? Do you think they were singing simply because they were bored? Not so fast.

New research is showing that working out (or physical effort, period) seems easier while producing music, hence the phrase, "whistle while you work."

The study, published in the Proceedings of the National Academy of Science USA, found that singing, humming, or whistling all made exercise easier by activating the center of emotional motor control in the brain. This area is responsible for spontaneous actions such as smiling and deliberate motor control. By activating this efficient brain system, you'll find exercise easier to engage in, and will be more likely to enjoy the time while you are.

It's not likely that Larry D. Barnes was aware of the science of humming and singing in terms of the impact it had on the human brain in the 1970's. Yet, Larry often told me about how he would sing aloud in his car, first thing in the morning, and from the house of one prospective client to the next. Larry would frequently tell me, "My voice was a powerful tool!" He had a deep intuitional understanding about the impact the sound, tone, and volume of his speaking voice had on those he was talking to.

Scientists now tell us that the area of the brain that processes sounds, called the auditory cortex, and the area processing feelings, called the kinesthetic cortex, overlap by about forty percent. In short, this means that sounds and feelings really aren't all that much different. The sound of our voice, very literally influences how the people we are speaking to, feel, for better, or for worse.

What Larry might not have known, however, was the boost that singing to himself was giving him. It was a circle of success begetting success; the more Larry sang, the more he activated the center of emotional control, and the more he activated this area of his brain, the easier it was for him to focus, and do the work required of him as an insurance agent whose success depended largely on his level of self-discipline.

All the while, his singing was also keeping his vocal cords loose and limber, allowing him to deliver his presentations in an eloquent tone that drew people closer to him.

One of the things that set Larry apart from his peers was his keen awareness of the things that made a positive difference in his life. Having the wherewithal to stop and reflect, to look back on each day and ask, "What things did I do today that worked well, that helped me move closer to my desired outcomes?" How many people do you think arbitrarily sang on the way to an appointment, but failed to make the connection between their warmer tone of voice and the favorable outcome of the sales experience?

If you aren't aware of what you are doing, and the results that are being created, it's going to be almost impossible to consciously craft your actions each day, refining your behaviors and actions and getting sharper and more proficient in your profession or chosen career. This is one place that Larry was different. He did reflect. He did observe. He did pay attention, and he did learn and apply on an ongoing basis.

One of the most important points, regarding Larry's application of this simple process of singing to himself to warm up his voice before a sales call, is that he didn't need to have hard science backing him up on the merits of singing to warm your voice, and how that would be useful as an insurance agent.

All he needed was the feedback offered when he simply paid attention to what was going on around him. What was working, and what wasn't. He dropped what wasn't working, and did more of what was.

My Thoughts and Reflections on the Section I Just Read

The Power of Goals

"If you're bored with life - you don't get up every morning with a burning desire to do things - you don't have enough goals."

—Lou Holtz

One hot July afternoon, while sipping a glass of peach tea listening to Larry D. Barnes smoothly transition from one enthralling story to another, I readied myself for a question I had long wanted to ask. I carefully sat my tea down on the glass-top dining room table, the "clack" from the two glass surfaces making contact serving as an auditory marker of where one thought had finished, and where another was about to begin.

"Larry," I asked, as I placed my pen down next to my legal pad, "Has there ever been anything that you wanted, that you didn't have?" Larry fixed his eyes, having them aimed at a spot that seemed to be about ten feet behind me, as his slightly defocused eyes appeared to be looking right through me. He sat quietly for what seemed like five minutes, but in truth was probably more like twenty seconds of silence so quiet that I could hear us both breathing. Suddenly, his focus sharpened, pulling his attention back to me, and moving his eyes up to meet mine. "No, I can't think of anything I've ever wanted that I haven't had. If there is something, I've forgotten it."

Think of it. A man with seven decades behind him, almost

eight, and he can't think of anything he's ever wanted that he hasn't had. I had never asked that question of anyone else, of any age, and gotten that answer. It's quite a remarkable thing, actually, especially when you think of all of the things that he has had, done, or experienced. It's not as though he had lived some Zen like existence, content just to exist, and thrive on hours of meditation while seated on some distant mountain top. He's lived aggressively. Larry dreamed big, and went well beyond the norm in his thinking about what he wanted to have or experience in his lifetime.

When one considers the marvelous reality of someone having had or experienced everything they want in life, it warrants asking the question, "What is the secret to having everything you want?" To be able to get to the end of your life and realize you've had everything you ever wanted.

When I asked Larry this question, his answer came in a steady, even metered tempo. His words flowed so smoothly that they almost had a musical quality to them. "The secret of having had everything I ever wanted, sadly, isn't a secret. It's a principle that has been around for a long time, and has proved itself over and over again. Yet, it is still largely ignored by most people. Creating goals for myself and being clear about what I wanted created a fortune for me. It allowed me to have everything I ever wanted. Goal setting is the key to getting anything you want in life."

Larry laid out the following steps that he suggested anyone could use to create the life of their dreams, just as he had done for himself.

Larry's Goal System:

1. Decide what you want.
   Define it in as much detail as possible.

2. Write down exactly what you intend to give back in exchange for what you receive or experience.

3. Write down the intended date for which you will have the experience you desire.

4. Take everything you have written down in steps 1-3, and write at least a paragraph describing what you want, what you intend to give back, and where, when, and how you plan to experience the achievement of this goal. Use rich and emotionally loaded words to create an intense visual landscape that will give your mind a clear picture to focus on.

One afternoon while we were talking about the subject of goals, Larry leaned forward in the black leather recliner he'd been relaxing in while we were chatting. He reached over to the small wooden table just to the left of his chair, grabbed his notebook, and picked up one of his "Larry D. Barnes" black and silver pens he loved to give away to friends and neighbors, and started to draw the chart below (his comments made while drawing are on the following page):

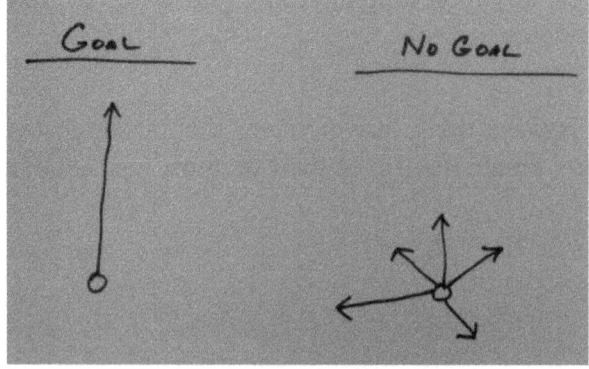

"The best way I know to show the importance of goals is to show this simple drawing," he told me as he started writing. On the upper left hand side, he wrote "Goal," on the upper right hand side, he wrote "No Goal." About four inches beneath the word "Goal" on the left side of the page, he drew a small circle and a straight line going from that circle, directly to the word "Goal."

On the right hand side, about four inches beneath the words "No Goal," he drew a circle. This circle, however, had lines coming out from all sides of the circle. Some went from the top of the circle towards the words "No Goal," but most of the lines went in other directions, directions away from the words "No Goal."

"This is what happens," Larry said in earnest, "when you have a goal!" He was pointing at the single straight line on the left side of the page that went directly to the word "Goal." He went on, "And this is what happens when you don't have goals. Your decisions go every which way, most of them ending up nowhere useful. You simply cannot make good decisions unless you have a goal. With no goal, with nothing to aim for, you just can't work or think efficiently!"

Larry's pen was moving back and forth, from one side of the paper to the other. "Every day we make thousands of decisions. Most of them we aren't even aware of. These are decisions about what to eat, what to wear, where we are going, when we are going, and whether we are going by ourselves, or with someone.

Our day is full of decisions that we have to make, and having a goal lets us know immediately whether the decision we are about to make will take us closer to our goal, or not. With goals, decisions are made much more easily. Successful people make decisions quickly, and change them, if at all, very slowly. Unsuccessful people make decisions very slowly, and change them quickly and many times. They have to, because without a goal, they have no idea which—if any—of their decisions is a useful decision."

You may, or may not realize what you have with Larry's system. You have a clear cut and, more importantly, time tested system for acquiring anything, or having almost any experience in life that you would like to have. Does that seem like an exaggeration? Does that sound like a trumped up claim like those you might hear on a late night infomercial? Ask Larry D. Barnes what he thinks about that.

My Thoughts and Reflections on the Section I Just Read

INSIGHTS FROM THE WRITINGS OF LARRY D. BARNES

The following thoughts and insights were recorded over the years by Larry, in various journals and notebooks

"When you think about investments and you don't consider the tax effect on results, you have missed getting max results. You must know both investments and taxes to get results you want."

"To keep your mind sharp, you must exercise your mind with challenging decisions."

"Independence is achieved by making yourself more effective in taking care of all your needs—learn how to do all these things."

"Fishing does not deplete your time on earth—that time is added to your lifetime."

"Questions are the secret to learning from others experiences."

"If you are goal oriented, you will make decisions fast and change your mind slowly. A goal directed person makes decisions quickly because he knows what he wants."

"Desire is a trait you cannot test to determine, but it is the most important trait to success. Medium talent and great desire will beat great talents and low desire."

"The feelings you get when you do someone a favor are so fantastic."

"Love creates energy that you can channel several different ways—this energy needs to be used."

"You make things happen for the good when you get out of your comfort level and step out to achieve. Sometimes you will fail, but often you succeed. The poor soul who always stays in his comfort level never knows the excitement of achieving more in life."

"If you get mad you lose. Always keep control of your feelings so you can make wise decisions."

"You get what you want in life, so make sure you know (for certain) what you want."

"Keep your eye on your goal and you can make decisions to draw your goal to you."

"The Christian must always keep his mind on Christ as his or her example, never achieving a Christ-like position, but working on the right decision."

"Jesus said the most important commandment is love. Love yourself as you do your neighbor. Love is from God—love God with all your might."

"Once saved, always saved is good news to all sinners."

"If you share love, you double it. If you share your problems with a friend, you cut your problems in half."

"Use it or lose it, as a philosophy, not only pertains to your talents, but every phase of your Christian life."

"God loves me. This is the greatest fact you can ever know. He does, you know."

"Since God has been removed from our schools and businesses, I have never seen so many troubles—terrorists, world disasters, shootings etc. Think about this and remember to pray for reversal of this problem."

"To be successful financially you must: 1. Put yourself in a position to grow. 2. Learn the basics of what you are doing extremely well and apply your efforts towards a goal.
Goals are necessary to make wise decisions."

"The golden rule is so simple, and yet, so many ignore it when they go about their daily tasks."

"Do the things you don't like to do, but are necessary to accomplish your goals. Soon, you will find you do these things well and you like to do them. The average person doesn't do this. Do you want to be average? I don't think so. Average is the worst of the best and the best of the worst."

"You want to do the best for your family. Don't forget to share quality time with them."

"Love your competition. They give you drive to excel and keep you sharp."

"There is no test you can give to measure desire. Therefore, I didn't test anyone who expressed an interest to go to work for me. If I couldn't think of a reason to not hire them, I contracted them."

"I personally don't see how anyone can accomplish anything in life without a strong spiritual life."

"The book 'Think and Grow Rich' and the accompanying 'Action Pack' is the very best motivation book ever written, in my opinion. Get it, read it, study it, apply it, and I think you will agree."

WORDS OF PRAISE FOR LARRY D. BARNES

"The mediocre teacher tells. The good teacher explains. The superior teacher demonstrates. The great teacher inspires."

-William Arthur Ward

Dan McNerney
Founder of MMG, Inc.

When I sat down to write something that would adequately reflect my gratitude for the many ways in which Larry D. Barnes influenced my life, I knew it would be difficult to condense it to just a page or two. In fact, that can't be done; all I can do is express as much as I can, as succinctly as possible, and let the reader know, that for whatever I have written, there is so much more that will forever remain in my heart and soul.

Larry gave me an opportunity to experience a life that was so far beyond my ability to imagine when I first started in the insurance industry, that even looking back on what I've experienced, can at times, seem surreal.

Of course, it's easy to get caught up in the financial aspect of what my time with Larry D. Barnes provided for my family. There were things that aren't so easily appraised, though, in terms of their worth. Things that aren't as tangible; things that, in truth, aren't really "things". They are ideas, values and concepts for living a life that will allow you to one day exit this earthly existence, and be proud of the legacy you are leaving behind.

Larry D. Barnes taught me about the importance of giving someone your word. The idea that other people could have enough faith to move forward on what you have promised, simply because you have made that promise. Larry D. Barnes taught me about the importance of immersing yourself in your work, while you were working. No one lived and breathed insurance like Larry. He was not easily distracted, because he had such clearly defined goals for what he wanted to have happen for the agency the next week, the next month and the next year. Larry got up thinking about how he could make the agency a better place, and drove home each night, still thinking about what he could do to improve the agency that carried his name.

I learned about the importance of sharing your success with your family, from Larry. Larry felt that it was wrong for a man to earn a significant income and not share it with his family. I saw the joy Larry got from seeing loved ones benefit from his efforts, and I feel very blessed to be able to say I have felt that joy, in my own life, having been able to see how my efforts have allowed my own family to experience things that not everyone is able to enjoy.

When I expressed my interest in the position of becoming the state manager, when Larry announced that he would soon be creating this new title, I was told what I needed to do to be considered. I did what was asked of me, and as promised, I was given the opportunity to work in a very close capacity with Larry for several years. It was an experience that would help shape me for one day running my own company as successfully as Larry D. Barnes ran his.

To say that Larry D. Barnes has touched many lives would be an understatement. Larry served as a role model for living, not only a successful life, but a fulfilled life. There is a difference between the two. Both are important, but to be successful without also being fulfilled is an empty existence. Larry knew this, and vigorously promoted the idea of accomplishing both. A fulfilling life, is one that has served others, and served the greater good. A life that will leave the world in a better place than we found it. This was important to Larry, and he masterfully wove it through everything he taught, and through every goal he set.

The world is a better place because of Larry D. Barnes, without question, and one day, when it is my turn to leave this earth, and others are gracious enough to say the same about me, just know that Larry D. Barnes had a hand in the life I lived, and the legacy I left behind.

Matt Vaughn
Insurance Agent

When I graduated high school in 1984, I went to work for the Larry D. Barnes Insurance Agency. The day I started, I had parked my brand new Toyota Celica on the south end of the building, just outside of the door that served as an exit from Larry's office.

I had just climbed out of my car, when I heard a stern "Who's car is this?" bellowing from just a few feet away. "It's mine!" I said, as Larry continued walking down the steps. "Do you work for me?" Larry asked. "I sure do. I started today!" I told him. He welcomed me to the agency, complimented me on my car, and he was off.

Larry D. Barnes made it simple for anyone who was willing to work hard, to become as successful as they wanted to. From my very first day, it was clear that Larry's years of experience as a top producer himself, had been channeled into creating a template for others to follow. No one needed to re-create the wheel (although many would try and fail). Larry had taken the guess work out of selling insurance. If you followed Larry's system, and had thick enough skin to endure the "No's" that were a constant part of the day to day insurance business, you would do well.

Larry D. Barnes led by example; he exemplified leadership, through his walk, his speech, his appearance and his demeanor. When you walked into the Larry D. Barnes Insurance Agency, it would not have mattered if you had just moved to town, when you saw Larry, you knew he was at the helm. His leadership was instrumental, not only in the success of the agency, but in the individual success of many agents, like myself.

Today, when I take a moment to step back and look at the life I live, and what I get to experience, it's simply not possible to think about it without also thinking of Larry D. Barnes. I will always be grateful for the opportunity he provided, and the leadership and inspiration that served to keep me moving forward.

Margaret Munday
Larry's Personal Secretary

I worked for Larry D. Barnes for nearly twenty years. I was his private secretary and bookkeeper, for both of his corporations. When my mother was dying from cancer, he gave me over a month off work to be with her, and paid me for every single day.

He was always giving the staff gifts. We all went out to lunch together every Friday, on Larry. There were large Christmas bonuses every year, yearly raises and great working conditions. Our offices were beautiful. The co-workers were great, too. It was like having a second family. When Larry sold his agency and decided to retire, he gave all the staff a fifty-thousand dollar check.

I learned so much working with Larry, going from a manual typewriter and paper accounting to data bases, word processing programs and computer accounting programs.

It was fun working for Larry—instead of a "job". He was the most kind, generous, compassionate and understanding boss anyone could ever have; and a good Christian man. Larry D. Barnes, was, and still is, a very classy guy!

Robert "Bob" Barnes
Assure Missouri & Associates, Inc.

Thank you for the offer to give my thoughts about Larry D Barnes.

It is impossible to be around Larry D. Barnes and not have some of his positive enthusiasm and zeal rub off on you. He is relentless about the things that he believes in and is fast in getting others involved in his pursuit.

I had been out of high school a few years and gotten into the building trade like the three generations before me. One weekend in 1974 I was visiting my parents. My father said that Larry D. Barnes had moved to Trenton. Larry had a new business opening in Trenton and I should go by and say "Hi."

"Larry D. Barnes Insurance" was painted in big letters on the building window and Larry had a razor blade scrapping off the over spray from the windows when I arrived. We talked outside for a while then he invited me in. He had some things that required a pen and pad to explain. I had no idea at that time that my life was about to take a new direction.

By February of the following year I had completed and passed the state insurance test and was in the insurance business. Presently, I am in my 39th year of my insurance career.

When I started, Larry liked to meet in the mornings before work and have coffee. This was great for me, new in the business, to go over yesterday and plan for the day. One particular morning Larry and I met at the College Inn restaurant for coffee and he introduced me to a pretty little waitress that I have now been married to for over 37 years.

Larry encourages and promotes people through his confidence and respect for them and their often hidden abilities. He has the ability to recognize and ignite that ember of desire in people into a blazing inferno.

As you can tell I have many thankful thoughts about Larry. I will always be in his debt.

Bobby Dean Richardson
Co-President, MMG, Inc.

When thinking about Larry D. Barnes and the influence that he has had on my life and career, I have to tell you a story of how I got to know Larry. In July of 1980 I had a opportunity to meet with Larry in his office in Trenton, Missouri, for a formal interview to talk about the career as an insurance agent. I came to this interview having just gotten married in May of that year, and was currently working for a lumber company, as a yard foreman.

I was looking for a career that could lead me to where I could build a business which would allow me to could control my own destiny, rather than allowing others to control it for me.

As I walked into Larry's office that day, I was thinking in my mind that insurance sales and the commission-only pay, was probably not going to be the career path that I was going to follow, but I was going to explore all options that were available to me . Larry was very professionally dressed and had a very contagious smile on his face, as he extended his hand to welcome me that day .

Larry asked a lot of questions to get me talking about myself so he could get to know me and understand what I was looking for in a career. "Seek to understand before trying to be understood" was the first lesson I learned that day from Larry. After Larry got to understand me and where I was coming from, he spoke the following words; words I will never forget: "Bobby let me show you what the average man wants."

He was honest and hit the nail directly on the head, showing me what life could hold for me if I was to simply ask for it and commit myself to what I really wanted out of life . It wasn't about selling insurance; it was about the vision and the confidence in myself, and that was what Larry D. Barnes was able to bring out in me that day . Larry had the ability to find the good in me, and help me believe in myself and believe that I could, and should, have all the things in life that I wanted .

Not very often in life do you meet an individual that can have the kind of a impact on your life that Larry had on mine that day. I was twenty-one years old at that time and was very lucky to have met Larry D. Barnes that day. Not only did he inspire me, but it continued for several years following. He was a man that cared about not only me, but also my family . I still, to this day, share lessons of life that I not only was told by Larry, but was also shown by the way he lead his life . It wasn't about selling insurance that day, it was about LIFE.

Thirty-four years later I'm still in the insurance profession and currently President of MMG Inc. in Columbia, Missouri. My wife Debbie and I very often talk about that day back in 1980, and are very thankful for getting to know Larry D. Barnes in the way that we were able to. To say that Larry had a major influence on my career is one thing; but the real impact of Larry D. Barnes on my life is measured by the way he continues to influence the way I live and think, and this speaks volumes about the kind of man he is, and the impact his life has had on others.

We all need to meet an individual like Larry D. Barnes in our life, and because of the influence that Larry had on me, I have always tried to be that type of man to others.

Alan Ferguson
Barnes & Baker Automotive, Salesman, and Former Agent with the Larry D. Barnes Insurance Agency

I don't know where to begin when asked to talk about the influence that Larry D. Barnes has had in my life and my career. There is not a day that goes by that I don't hear his voice in the back of my head when I'm working with a customer. The basic fundamentals of selling are skills that do not get taught today and are skills that we need more than ever!

Over the years in my sales career, I have leaned heavily on the fact that your job, and life in general are 90% attitude, and that you can accomplish anything that you believe you can! I was always amazed at the fact that when we had a sales meeting, and Larry would speak, how the entire room would listen like he was E.F. Hutten. I can still hear him telling the "average man" story.

I always found it interesting how even when you had a tough week, Larry would be able to take you right back to the basics and mentally prepare you for another week, and get you to realize that sales was a numbers game, and to get back in there and keep swingin' the bat. Amazingly, it would work.

I don't know how many times I have heard his voice say "the

best time to sell a policy is right after you just sold one. Your enthusiasm is high and your skills are sharpest right then, so go knock on another door," or "If you don't have an appointment for tomorrow you are unemployed so always try to have one or more planned for 9:00 am sharp!"

I have also always remembered the importance of a good presentation and how important it is to involve your customer in that presentation and how that helps to build value in your product or service. I have always tried to continue to learn because I can remember Larry telling us that everyone, for the most part, is worth the same amount of money from the neck down. It's what you've got from the neck up that they'll pay you more money for, and the more you know and are willing to apply, the more you'll make.

He also always told us that if we could get good at selling insurance we could sell anything well because it is an intangible product, and that is exactly right. I could literally go on for hours with stories that involve Larry and the influence that he had in my life and career and I'm sure to a lot of people that know him, they would sound very familiar, because he was also the king of repetition and how that was the best way to learn something. Do it twenty-one times and from there on it's a habit and becomes a part of you. That has definitely worked for me over the years .

In closing, I am very grateful to Larry for the opportunity to have worked for him and to call him a friend, mentor and most of all a Brother in Christ! I look forward to many more good times as the years keep flying by. Thanks again and again!

P. S. 10-5-3-1. Only select people will understand those numbers…

Cindy McCracken
Editor of the Weekly Newsletter, Larry D. Barnes Insurance Agency

I was privileged to be able to work for Larry. D. Barnes during an exciting period of phenomenal growth. A big and extremely rewarding part of my job was designing the weekly newsletter. It reflected the accomplishments of the amazing work the agents were doing each week out in the field, and how the influence of the Larry D. Barnes Insurance Agency grew by leaps and bounds each week.

Larry was a very sincere and authentic man to work for. His leadership skills and abilities were the backbone of the agency. He was well respected, and that was simple to understand; he respected each of us, and treated us like co-workers, as part of his team, and not just employees.

In the years since I worked for Larry, I've often thought of what wonderful years those were, and how well he took care of us, and the dedication he showed, not only to the agency that held his name, but to the people who made things happen behind the scenes.

At every turn, Larry went out of his way to recognize us, and to make sure we knew how much he appreciated our hard work. He did those simple things that so many people forget to do. He made eye contact with us when you were speaking to him. He called us by name, because he knew our names. In short, he made us feel important.

Polly Applebury
Former V.P. of Marketing for Larry D. Barnes

When you are young and first getting started in your career, oftentimes the enthusiasm and drive to succeed you bring to a new job is quickly dampened by the day to day activities of what the job actually turns into. However, I was fortunate enough early in my life to secure a job with the Larry D. Barnes Agency.

In the halls of a Larry D. Barnes business, you always saw happiness and enjoyment in the workplace. Larry expected high performance from his team, but he provided us with the tools to be able to reach and exceed the expectations he set. Larry knew how to create an open work environment where you felt comfortable enough to share your thoughts and opinions.

With good communication being a high priority within his business, Larry always took the time to listen and was open to any suggestions. He allowed you to be creative and to think outside the box, and always expressed his praise and showed his gratitude when we did.

Larry was the head of one of the fastest growing insurance agencies around and was very successful. While he enjoyed wearing expensive suits, perfectly polished shoes and a stylish watch, he treated everyone he came into contact with as an equal. Larry also shared his success with the community. He took the time to make sure that those around him were fed spiritually and with love.

Larry never wanted what he did for others to be known, or a big deal made of it. When I think back over my time with Larry I am amazed when I recall all the things he did for others during that time period.

I use Larry's mannerisms every day. I will never forget how he carried himself around others. The confidence, kindness, and calmness he displayed are the marks of a true gentleman. His non-verbal messages were just as powerful as his verbal messages. His body language seemed to say "Speak up, but be nice, speak up, but talk educated, speak up and back up your statements with facts." Daily, Larry walked this walk.

After working for years at the Larry D Barnes Agency, Larry asked if I would like to start a new business with him and of course I said "Yes!" Helping Larry start Successful Sales System, Inc. was the opportunity of a lifetime for me. I once read the following quote, "Encourage and reward your employees, without them, you can do nothing. They help you accomplish your goals; now help them accomplish theirs". This is exactly what Larry did for me and so many others.

At Successful Sales System, Inc. I was the V.P. of Marketing for many years. Larry mentored me and gave me the opportunity, direction and the freedom I needed to succeed. Because of his training and leadership I developed a strong sense of self-confidence and his constant encouragement made me set and reach even higher goals. Because of the knowledge he shared, the risks he took and the investment he made in each of his employees, we were able to leave with the tools necessary to succeed in today's world. I'm not just talking money, but the knowledge of the day to day operations of how to do business right.

However, Larry was not just all about the business. Larry also understood that we all had personal lives and he went out of his way to embrace that part of our lives. When my first child arrived, I was able to take him to work with me for the first six months of his life. Larry understood the value of family.

The years I spent with Larry D. Barnes are a chapter in my life I recall with much joy. It is a chapter that made me develop into what I am today. I appreciate you, Larry, for the kindness and support you showed me and my family. Thank you for allowing me to be a part of everything. I miss the business and I miss you, Larry! I miss the morning visits and all the lunches Larry was always treating the staff to. (I also miss those bonus checks!)

I will close with the following. It's something I picked up from Larry and had on my bulletin board during the years I worked for him:

How to become successful:

1. Position yourself

2. Learn basics

3. Goal set with action

4. Follow instructions

Larry D. Barnes made a difference in my life and the lives of so many others. May we all aspire to have the kind of impact on the world that Larry D. Barnes has had.

Terri Henderson
Entrepreneur & Owner of Chic Salvage

In the late 1970s, I was helping feed our cattle as an old, green truck pulled in our drive. Living on a farm, a visitor was a big deal. Out of the truck came a man that my parents went to high school with that I would later learn was Larry Barnes. His blue jeans were cuffed at the bottom and did not look like they had been worn much. He looked like what we called a hobby farmer. When school started a few weeks later, I was introduced to my locker mate, Diane Barnes. We became fast friends, and I found out that she was the daughter of the guy who had come to our farm in the old, green truck to buy some hay from my dad.

Both Diane and I got out of school to work in the afternoons, and most days we would meet Larry for lunch at a local restaurant called The Crown. Each day, as we met and visited, I remember being shocked at how differently he dressed than my dad. His hands did not have grease under his fingernails. I soon learned that he was starting an insurance agency that was growing by leaps and bounds.

Larry was very interesting to visit with and seemed very interested in what Diane and I were doing in school, as well as our jobs. It seemed like each week, his insurance company was hiring more and more agents. I was not sure how they were growing so quickly, but I knew that he must be doing something right. Talking with Larry was an uplifting experience, as well as being humorous. He made both Diane and I believe that we could accomplish anything that we wanted to achieve.

At age 21, I was given an opportunity to purchase my first business. I thought back on high school conversations with Larry during lunch at The Crown. I just knew that I would be successful. Back in those days, there were no seminars, webinars, and very few books on entrepreneurship. Basically, one could be successful in business if he or she worked hard, learned from the best in the business, and followed business ethics.

Larry's approach to business was very aggressive in what he believed that he could do. I used some of the tips that I learned from him to grow my business into a highly successful one that turned a profit for decades.

During my 20s, I had an opportunity to take a lead role in a fundraising campaign in our town. Also, taking a very key role was none other than Larry Barnes. I just knew that we could work together as a team to achieve some very aggressive targets that were set for our group. Larry used the same set of skills that he used to grow his business to gain momentum for our fundraising campaign. His endorsement and enthusiasm helped others to believe that our cause was a good one to get involved in.

As a non-traditional student in college, I chose to major in history and minor in political science. After having learned about the political process in a book, I thought that it would be fun to run for political office in our town even though few women had ever held political office.

Much to my dismay, my opponent and the incumbent, got an endorsement from Larry and was able to utilize the phone system at his office for making calls to voters. Unfortunately, I lost by a slim margin. Not to be deterred by defeat, I ran the next year as well. But before putting my name on the ballot, I went to visit with Larry and asked if I could count on his support this time and asked why he had not supported me in the previous election. He said "I did not support you because you never asked." Thankfully, I won the next election by a wide margin, and served three terms in office.

In watching Larry for over the past 40 years, I believe what sets him apart from other entrepreneurs is his philanthropic nature. He has given countless dollars to our community and has challenged others to do the same. He has left many legacies in our community and has encouraged many prospective business owners.

As I see the tall steeple on the First Baptist Church each evening during sunset, a gift from Larry D. Barnes to our community, I am reminded that we should not let the sun set on any day without working hard, encouraging others, and leaving a legacy for generations to come. One can start out in cuffed up blue jeans and an old, green pickup and reach heights far beyond what anyone can imagine.

Philip and Leah Helton
Helton Insurance Agency

I met Larry D. Barnes in 1979, and again in early 1980. At that time you could sell insurance with just a six month permit (without an insurance license).

"Mr. Insurance," as Larry was known in Trenton at that time, inspired many people. His approach to the business brought a whole new concept to selling insurance. He could capture an audience and the mind of an insurance agent, with his way of handling people. He used his charm and speaking ability, and presented and persuaded people in a way that really struck me, and I wanted to learn from him. Most meetings and outings seemed to hold a "Christian Attitude".

Larry always wanted the best, not only for himself but for those around him. He told me it pleased him a great deal to see others that worked with him, becoming successful in their own business.

Leah and I want to thank Larry D. Barnes for giving us the opportunity to earn and make a living in the insurance business the last 35 years.

Final Thoughts from the Author

In 2008, Larry D. Barnes would face the biggest challenge of his life; an experience that would come very close to claiming his life. Born from an unfortunate and largely unavoidable turn of events, Larry's once vibrant health would quickly take a nose dive. His heart would stop beating, and be medically started again, a total of six times. He would ultimately have a pacemaker put in to keep his damaged heart beating rhythmically.

He would have an emergency tracheotomy performed, not once, but three times, and was placed on a life sustaining respirator a total of four times. Larry would get an ileostomy after a seven hour exploratory surgery where most of his colon and intestines were removed, and his kidney function would cease, resulting in the three times per week kidney dialysis he is doing, even as I write, and will, for the rest of his life.

As Larry approaches his seventy-eighth birthday, his mind is still as sharp as a tack. The last six years have taken a toll on him physically, to be sure, but Larry still has a knack for being able to focus on what he can do, and not allowing himself to be pulled down by dwelling on the things he can no longer do.

I think about the June, 2014 afternoon, when Larry, myself and my daughter, Chloe went out fishing on his bass boat. Gone were the days where he could prepare the boat and get it launched from the dock, himself. Yet, Larry seemed to take great satisfaction in showing me what to do. He wasn't about to throw in the towel and stop fishing just because he couldn't do everything he used to do. He simply settled into a role that was feasible, given his physical condition, and kept moving forward in true Larry D. Barnes fashion.

After we had cleared the dock, cast the first lines and brought in the first fish of the day, a focused hush surrounded the boat like some invisible orb of peace. Few words were spoken. Larry was no longer watching the beauty of the day around him; Larry had-as much as one can-become one with the beauty of the day.

His breathing was no longer labored and there was no sign of physical pain or fatigue. A relaxed look had settled in on his face, seemingly smoothing out the lines of the last seventy-seven years, and the stress of the last five or six of those years. For as much as Larry is known for his business ventures and ability to make money, I caught a glimpse of him in another element of love.

Henry David Thoreau perhaps said it best: "Many men go fishing all of their lives without knowing that it is not fish they are after." Oh, Larry loved catching fish, and was just as fond of eating the fish he caught, but he knew there was a dimension of fishing that couldn't be measured. In fact, it couldn't even been seen with the naked eye. It could only be felt. I think this sums up Larry's life. He knows that what really matters at the end of the day, or at the end of a life, are the moments, memories and experiences that move us deeply—those things that cause a visceral response that we feel at the inner most depths of our gut, and our heart. Fishing, for Larry, I believe, is a metaphor for a life well lived, and that, my friend, is how Larry D. Barnes has lived his life.

I spent the better part of a year with Larry D. Barnes, talking with him several hours each week, peeling back the layers of his psyche and asking questions that would trigger long forgotten memories, so I could discover the many ways in which he touched the lives of others. Along the way, I had an awakening of sorts; I knew I was no longer searching for that answer, because I had experienced it myself. Without the conscious intention of doing so, I had allowed Larry D. Barnes to weave his magic through the tapestry of my own life, and for that experience, I will be forever thankful.

CONTRIBUTIONS TO THE COMMUNITY

Larry D. Barnes never saw the accumulation of money as the end goal. The wealth he created was viewed as a tool; a tool that allowed more choices in life. One of those choices, was the ability to look at his community, and decide where he would like to use his wealth to help create a better place for others to live.

Two particular contributions, warrant mentioning, here. They are not mentioned, merely because of the amount of money involved; they simply represent two of the donations that have the widest impact on the greatest number of people, both of which were also very near and dear to Larry's heart.

North Central Missouri College, Trenton, MO:
Cash and real estate donations totaling in excess of $500,000

First Baptist Church, Trenton, MO:
Several donations totaling approximately $640,000

CHRONOLOGICAL HISTORY

Significant Events in the Life of Larry D. Barnes

Born: October 6th, 1936

Graduated High School, 1954

Enlisted in the United States Army, 1955

Married Coleen Crawford, 1956

Honorable discharge from United States Army, 1957

Employed two months at Mart's Drug, Trenton, MO, 1957

Employed by Gamble's, Trenton, MO, 1957

First child born-Debra Elaine, 1957

Second child born-Lynda Diane, 1959

Third child born-Larry Dewayne, 1960

Promoted to Store Manager at Gamble's, 1961

Moved to manage largest Gamble's store in district, 1962

Employed as Insurance Agent with MFA,
District Sales Manager, 1966

Promoted to State Manager, MFA, 1974

Regional Manager, Standard Life Insurance, 1974

Started Larry D. Barnes Insurance Agency, in Trenton, MO, 1975

Sold the Larry D. Barnes Insurance Agency, first retirement, 1989

Started Successful Sales Brokerage, 1989

Sold Successful Sales Brokerage, second retirement, 1999

Almost lost his life to illness, 2008

www.ingramcontent.com/pod-product-compliance
Lightning Source LLC
Chambersburg PA
CBHW071731090426
42738CB00011B/2461